CAFE HAIKU

Text by Zenbu Nometa
Photography by Jeffrey Goldsmith

Caffeine Society
San Francisco

© 2004

Enjoy this moment.

No matter how still we sit,

time passes quickly.

Here's utopia.

Tables waiting everywhere.

Coffee piped in hot.

Hi there, Nicotine.

Would you like one? Oui, bien sur.

Devilish cafe friend.

An empty cakebox.

With your slice of nothingness.

You baked it for you.

One gives and one takes.

Register is mostly closed.

Tip jar is open.

Vonnegut put it:

Make characters want something.

Cold glass of water.

Ugh, tasteless neon.

But, hey, they've got hot coffee.

To go? No, we'll sit.

Dirty worn floorboards.

Light and shadow. Just surface?

Many shoes stepped here.

No one is playing.

Chess pieces need caffeine, too.

Motivate their moves!

It's okay. Be sweet.

Open your heart to the world.

Swing your metal flap.

Please widen sidewalks!

We'd have more coffee outside.

Taxes for great good.

Laptop in cafe.

Not a new experience.

Modern-day pencil.

I called to ask you.

Can you smell my coffee breath?

I can smell yours, too.

Swipe, strip, soap, wash, dry.

Cafe next door to laundry.

Drink coffee naked.

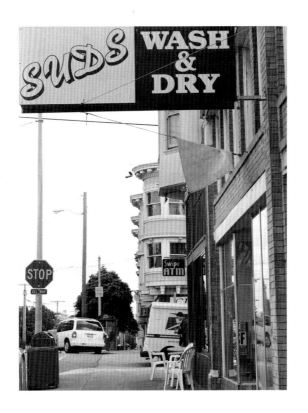

No refills in you.

Thrown away, stepped on, crushed.

Must it end this way?

Hot spigot on wheels.

You parked here. I came. It's fate.

Coffee truck coffee.

Yes, cops eat donuts.

And lattes, too. We all do.

We serve and protect.

Slowly savor sips.

Enjoy as you empty cup.

Life is delicious.

Sun always rises.

Here's a reason to get up.

Fill the chair's shadow.

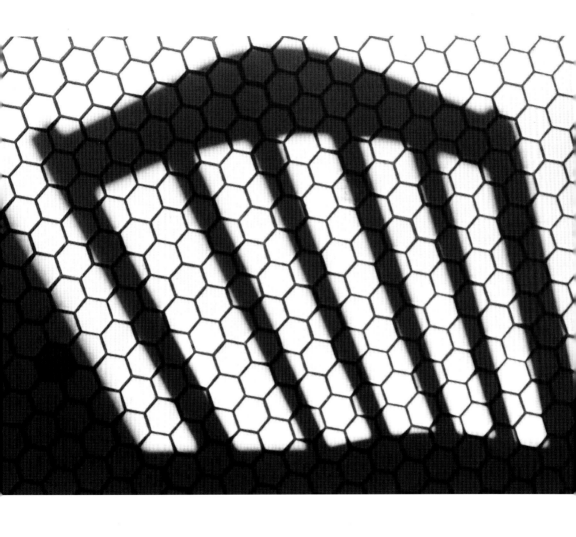

Yummy, I'm relieved.

Slice-of-chocolate-cake haiku.

My last meal is planned.

Rough smooth. Right texture.

Wood smell. Creamy brown color.

Raw beans in burlap.

Our hands still wander.

Desire inside blocks of glass.

The sound of the lid.

Upper shelf, pastries.

Middle shelf, cookies piled high.

Lower shelf, just crumbs.

Urns hold our coffee.

And urns are for our ashes.

A coincidence?

Stirring, the sticks say:

"If our tree foresaw its fate,

it would not have grown."

To cafes they go.

To talk of one thing most dear.

Michelangelo.

Cappuccino foam.

Creamy and sweetly bitter.

White with brown marbling.

Sweet however spelt.

Koffee is coffee.

Good all tymes of day.

You can reach right in.

Touch, smell, taste faraway lands.

Chocolate macaroon.

Programmers! Poets!

Mommies! Mechanics! Merchants!

We will serve you all.

How did the bark of

trees end up in a can we

sprinkle on milk foam?

Cockatoo cafe.

With capital and a concept,

open yours today!

Why just go Euro?

Vietnam's got great Java.

Condensed black and white.

Caffeine makes context.

This world radiates from you.

Mind expanding cup.

Oh, hello, again.

Why yesterday's like today.

Quotidian bean.

China on marble.

Textures do texture textures.

Turn milk into cream.

Go ahead. Add fat.

A cow ate grass so you could.

Photosynthesis.

Fun cafe or sad?

Love or hate? Good life or bad?

Thinking makes it so.

She scowled. Then sat down.

Nice legs! We try not to stare.

Sorry. I can't stop.

Reflections in sign.

Looking out a bus window,

much goes unnoticed.

People on the street.

Tra la la with their hot cups.

I asked them to stop.

Sex in a glass house.

Stirring for all the world to see.

An orgy of spoons.

What are they saying?

No one can hear their secrets.

Makes us curious.

Hiss, gurgle and drip.

Good things come to those who wait.

Hot cup of karma.

How sad. Glass empty.

It was good. And life is, too.

Order more of each!

Old worn wooden chair.

Zazen in light and shadows.

Meditate on it.

We read each other.

Not I, not you. You and I.

We wrote these haiku.

ZENBU NOMETA is a poet living in Shingu, Japan. Previously, he lived in New York for almost twenty years, before returning to run his family stationery shop. He studies the great poet, Issa.

JEFFREY GOLDSMITH resides in San Francisco, and grew up in Woodstock, NY. He has twice lived in Japan, and finds black and white images calligraphic. His work can be found at jeffreygoldsmith.com.